Love orange light warm

poems by

Jaclyn Alexander

Finishing Line Press
Georgetown, Kentucky

Love orange light warm

For Adina

(1986-2018)

Copyright © 2018 by Jaclyn Alexander
ISBN 978-1-63534-521-6 First Edition
All rights reserved under International and Pan-American Copyright Conventions. No part of this book may be reproduced in any manner whatsoever without written permission from the publisher, except in the case of brief quotations embodied in critical articles and reviews.

ACKNOWLEDGMENTS

Some of these poems have been previously published or are forthcoming in the following:

I-Phone notes 12:11 PM: *Prelude Magazine*
Then I was like: *Prelude Magazine*
To all the robot clowns: *Haribo*
Scissors to kiss: forthcoming in *Bowery Anthology*

Publisher: Leah Maines
Editor: Christen Kincaid
Cover Art: Joey Korein
Author Photo: Adnelly Marichal
Cover Design: Elizabeth Maines McCleavy

Printed in the USA on acid-free paper.
Order online: www.finishinglinepress.com
        also available on amazon.com

        Author inquiries and mail orders:
                Finishing Line Press
                  P. O. Box 1626
            Georgetown, Kentucky 40324
                      U. S. A.

Table of Contents

Me Too 1

Reading Lyn Hejinian's My Life 2

You are not in this room 3

In the middle of the sidewalk 4

No Fields Forever 5

We have no idea 6

Bells in the woods 7

Silver Tinsels 8

When I think about 9

I had a dream 10

I-phone notes, 12:11 PM 11

In the rain 13

What I want 14

First love 15

New Hampshire 16

To all the robot clowns 17

Loss is love 19

Tiny slices canyon solo 20

Then I was like 30

When the veil of sadness 31

Aftermath 32

Scissors to kiss 35

Me Too

We all want a love that is bigger than us, that will envelope us in a pool of safety, that will swallow us in warm orange light, but sometimes we find shards of glass between our toes.

Reading Lyn Hejinian's My Life

her deep thirst for moment yellow springs forth more memories. For breakfast we ate cream of wheat with salt and honey and called it mush. Blowing wish flowers and the tiny gray seeds sprinkling to the wind, pretending we are ragged soldiers and rationing the food on my dinner plate, yearning for a hearty stew, mom making crabs with melted butter, chocolate sodas in the summer, eating snow, tire swing deliriums, leaf piles, great uncle's magical carpet, fainting back on our beds, a summer counselor telling me I'll become a prostitute because I walk around naked constantly, using the word nympho not knowing what it means, my *Lands End* turquoise coat, a babysitter braiding our hair as we sat shirtless in overalls, her teaching us to draw flowers, wondering if I should hide in the washing machine, my uncle smoking a cigar under the stars. *One can run through the holes in memory, wearing a wet hat, onto the sidewalk covered in puddles, and there are fingers in them.* In the summer I watched a snake swallow a mouse. My father told me not to get too close to a squirrel that stared back at me, for it could have rabies.

You are not in this room

you are in a field of white snow,
the sky drips burning stars into you
Standing still in silence, a cold air blows from
a place you didn't know still existed

In the middle of the sidewalk

she drops to her knees
a thin man stares and walks by
only the trees watch her cry
as their leaves fall like spilled rice

No Fields Forever

write a poem of joy
a teacher instructed
lines read aloud
of yellow flowers
one tall languid yellow rose
sits at my window
sleek greened stem
leaning in confusion
misplaced
I can't turn off the noises in my head.
Screams of a young woman
locked in darkness,
breasts large,
nipples twisted with rusty pliers
forced naked on the ground
land of the free?
Sea to shining sea?
With justice and liberty for all?
I chose to be naked last night.
My freedom.
She didn't choose to be born
across the sea
he didn't choose to be born
at all.
Living is easy with eyes closed
another he sang.
Another she lives blindly in her garden—
my noise just won't stop
somehow it's hard to believe
there is one sun we all see

We have no idea

if we are just strange creatures
walking around in the minds of
ladybugs
and they are the little red queens of the earth
with the most knowledge
most complex language
and miniscule telescopes
in which they zoom in on us
and wonder at our strange babble

Bells in the woods

I don't want days to historicize my feelings
Picture lilies springing from my fingertips
Little particles little particles
Come from somewhere
My world is opening and closing
Do you want to come inside
my lily dream?

My life is a dream on rewind.

If you come we'll lie down facing the sky
and stars will drip into our eyes
I want you to understand time will cease
We will swallow the cool air
and lap the night over our tongues
Pull a zipper back and forth and jump inside

I will place dried flower petals all over your back

Oh, this sounds like a poem you have heard before
But we can be children again
walking underneath the trees we are shrinking
They are canopies over us: dark, wet, and plum

the sun knows
Squint-eyed your arm may stretch
to the moon

you may place your tears inside me
the color of our skin can drip into blue
and memory will be the word before yesterday

can we go there?
Is it possible to be inside my feeling
of bells ringing in the woods?

Silver tinsels

hang from straps of black leather
The Cocteau Twins are playing and women
shake their hips with violet eyes,
hair shaved off, heads different shapes.
Smells of coddled fish and wilted roses
It rained three days straight now
the sky is a smeared gray with purple tinges
The ground is wet,
water droplets
linger on flower petals

When I think about

how it didn't work
Sometimes
I want to stand in the ocean with you
Touch you for hours
It's so silly that we're both alive
And may never do this again

On the bright side
It was a reality check I needed
What delusional world was I living in
Where nobody would do anything like that
To me?

Yet one day you'll see me
And regret
Not letting me love you

I had a dream

about you last night
in it we were both alligators in bonnets
Get away from me you little salamander mush punk

You had a tiny miniature tongue growing in place
of one front tooth

"Practice makes perfect," you said.
"Practice makes bologna if you're making bologna," I said.

I-phone notes, 12:11 PM

Because you love you come undone
Strings unraveling out fly birds
nesting in your armpits strings
unspooling and close your eyes it
can be sex watercolor language the
seed of a pomegranate encased in
clear, it can be shitting as real
release of toxins and silly texts with
your friend you've known since
u were a kid and used to watch
Clockwork Orange in bed together no
threat of sexuality. Or maybe there
always was a wire of well, love
Now you send texts about
Freudian emotislips when he
accidentally sends you a heart
and laugh about it when you're high.
When you're high with old friends
language is slippery
as you stick your finger between
your friends' toes. You find new ways
of saying I love you so it feels real.
You've taken drugs with your old
friends where you both
became lions in the bathroom and a
boy shouted from outside the door
animal collective!
Vagina! Repeatedly.
Meanwhile the bathroom was vagina:
lavender, petals, lion women with whiskers.
anyway that was years ago and now
strings have unraveled and been
reformed. You've spent parts of your
life in rooms of different colors.

You've seen more of the shape of
your slippery celery dream (the
image that always returns)
Slipping into the abyss of tingles
Slowly
Dipping your feet after already
having drowned
She dropped a coin into the cup
Dylan sings
Now on your couch with a spoon of
peanut butter
Bath is running. You'll get in
eventually. Tonight you made up
several ideas: record listening party
watercolor party. you're
ready to yawn back into rooms of
warm orange light

In the rain

I lived in a cave of welled-off
darkness for some time

Ear-buds plugged in velvet
underground I'm beginning to see
the light.

I love you. What more is there to say.

I met myself in a dream
Child dreams rocks on eyes
Fish with legs and tiger fur

in my heart unspent it may explode

In the womb I started as two
In the class I started as silence
In the time I started as freedom
In age I moved to one
To noise
To cages
My words feel sparse
I hope you understand
There is so much I hope for
There is so much in this world that
makes me sink
In the rain now
the sadness is beautiful

What I want

To sink my bare-feet in warm wet soil
To run through fields laughing

First love

doesn't have the memory
of death attached

This is what makes all future love
different and perhaps
more beautiful

New Hampshire

I no longer want to eternally defer
        driving to Storm King on a given spring night
after we made pasta from scratch and
        just felt like it

if God is in us all is God in a can of tuna?
in factory waste?

To all the robot clowns

out there tryin'
hard just to live
Snorting come off a duck
There are no words to erase the
crinkle in the sheet
It's. Not every day u meet someone
whose eyes you want to look into
Call it the amalgam production of
our patriarchal capitalism the itch to
find comfort in a structure
Or call it humanity
Ink dripping perfusion lullaby
maelstrom inky squid lied butterfly
kiss salted cream when we were
running thru tires and swinging on
sprite pass the toenail clipper and
parched bottom like we were cool
but we weren't cool like we were
pink blossoms on the moon swelling
with heat and corruption like we
were tokens of bombed cities
Legs walking on earth out of a
garden
We all find ourselves here what are
we to do
In shriveled nails and sun
And some
it all made sense when we forgot we had
to leave
the exit blinked red as
we slipped into thighs spread with cake sighs
quivering icy ransack
Popsicle

I can't equate the thermos
of your spoon
to the inkblot of my
eye
i can't undermine the premise of
matter
I step on a shell made of we

loss is love

felt at a distance

Tiny slices canyon solo

For a long time
I was so inside loss
The world dripped with it

On the trail
Alone
The voices behind
Soothe me

River cool me
River cradle me
River carry me home

When you're really hot
There's nothing like
Dipping your head
In cold water

When you're really hungry
Sometimes
The right choice
Really is
a Snickers

my mind was so busy
I didn't even have
A moment
To realize

The fear
Of the mountain lion
Is different from
The fear
Of yourself

If lightning
Struck
Would I know what
To do?
Or would I crouch
Like a small child
And silently
Hope

Now by the river
Leaves stir
In the breeze
I'm
—

we passed
like currents
in one another's
lives
one day
I'll meet you at
the ocean

when I close my
eyes
I see
Ball of orange
Swirling pink
Wouldn't it be
Something
If we could all
Clasp hands

What
Are
Your
Dreams
In
This
One
Life?

There's a type
Of
Sadness
That cradles
You
To sleep
Like a
Lullaby

this sadness
is integral

Isn't it a shame
So many
Of us
Run around
With bogged dams
Of minds

I can't undo
What life I was
Born into
But
I can seek
To undo
Systemic
Injustice

When the levees broke
black bodies lay on
Top
Stacked like bricks
To hold up water

I sit
So small
At the bottom of
The canyon
As the fire ants
Sit
On me

I'm humbled
By
Stillness

When I noticed certain hairs
On my body
It's strange to recall
The first moment of
Becoming simultaneously
conscious
And
Self-conscious

Sometimes
After writing
I'm not sure
What to do
Next
And a lurch of
Loneliness
Settles in

Loneliness
Is so
Eternal
At times
It's
Holy

Joy
Is
Just
As
Eternal

Laughing in
Mud
Crying in
Seaweed

All of us searching
For a
Soul
To share
The dance with

I woke to your text
"People think I'm
nuts. I'm not nuts.
I just want to feel
It all."
(a miracle
Given I was at the
Bottom of the
Canyon)
And crossed
A shaky drawbridge

A hot wire of fear
Lurching through me
These are my fears
I tried to tell my mind
Counting numbers
Helped
Thank god I'm alone
I thought as I paused
Every now and then
And didn't dare
Look down
At the rushing
Colorado River
Murky brown in
It's course
The bridge began
To shake
More
And I thought
No it's in my
Head
At the end I released
A deep breath and
Looked back
To see
Three cowboy
Hatted men
Right behind me

I hadn't crossed alone
After all
But such grace
For them to remain
Silent
And allow me
To take my
Sweet
Time

The man who
Sold me my camel
Pack said
Don't be one of
Those people
Who carries a
Separate gallon
of water
Then he told me
It's pretty bad-ass
You're hiking alone
And yeah

I guess it is

Last night
I watched the sky smear
From bright blue
To midnight blue
And a sole star flickered
I don't normally
Allow
Fantastical narrations
Rooted in
Death
To linger too long
Inside
Perhaps because I'm
Superstitious
But this star
Was
My dead step-
Grandmother

Come down further
I whispered
And she did
We spoke about
My ailing grandpa
And when I said
Goodbye
She
Disappeared

It's starting to drizzle
I thought
God's tears
A lion's tail
Became a
Snake
Became a
Tree

Sometimes
The imagined lathering
Of your
Ego
Propels you

Thunder
Reminds you
Your ego
Can be
A
Fickle
Little
pickle

three cowboys
return

relief

The tree
Becomes a
Snake

They tell me
Last summer they hiked
Mt. Kilimanjaro
I ask if they've read
The Hemingway story
They ask if Hemingway
was a scientist

It's refreshing

Romansh sounds
Cradle me in a net
Of safety
As we march
Through the rain
Seek shelter under
A cliff

Don't
Let
Anyone
Steal
Your
Inner
Light

Then mist
Enshrouded the
Mountain
Like a vaginal
Womb

Cold shower exhaustion

Sometimes
It's good
To clean out
Your soul
Sorry to whoever
Smelled me today
I wasn't wearing deodorant

Cold shower elation

Then I was like

I.

Forget the
Wisp by and wrap your feet in it
Doesn't have to be the cello
feign when we were in broken pools
remember walking around
it was empty and
winter
you were in a smear of
a dog peed forever

II.

there was that man
on the train
some infection
arm bulbous
he kept grabbing his arm
stretching it out
trying to unstuck from inside
no way to escape a body
in this life
a child watched him in horror
fascinated
he cradled his arm as if it were
a loaf of bread
bulging over a pan
his face inescapable in knife
piercing the bread

and then we went for lemons and sweets
in the meadow
of our longing

When the veil of sadness

Lifts
What are you left with?
It's all dizzying
Caked hands you starched
Yesterday's morning with
You lifted flagpoles
      To wave over forgotten
Countries
      You whistled to a
      Deaf child
All to cling to a branch
      From the sky
      You couldn't see
When all that's let go
What will stir within?
What will blow the wind
Whip the leaves
Send your hair down
Clogged drains
When the veil is finally lifted
What will it all look like?

Aftermath

I.

for a moment
you're
lampooned in blank
it's worse than
sadness
it's an itch to remember
eyes

it's a cavern of
stuck inside
glass

tears find their way in
salt never abandoned
an ocean

yet,
no release

it's no words
—silence like smog

so a tear is
stapled to un-melting
ice

II.

to remember
(despite the glass)
sex
love
magic

freedom
warmth
orange
baths
showers
harmony
trust
shampoo
conditioner
suds
fields
skies
blues
lavenders
aqua
words
silence
sheets
air gasp

III.

H.D.
writes
of the jellyfish existence
the lurking swirls
the undulating sphere
an essence
of light
tinged in silver
scales of thin macabre
smoke
threads of hair
strands of silk

underneath inner
scooped in the bowl
of deep

each word a grasping
at the throttle
a clinging to
underneath
language
which isn't silence,

but song

Scissors to kiss

And then love pools in
That thirst for salt
The first adult falling in this bath
Of warm orange light:
rediscovery
So when the crescendo fades,
The branches stretch out even barer
Into forlorn gray skies, dried yellow
Leaves crunch under foot on a ground
That seems to hold
    nothing
At its center

Yet a secret nobody tells you as a child
Is nobody knows for certain magic doesn't exist
And if you believe
You're likely to find stars in your hand
So the power of your mind
Can transform stars into gold, milk into proverbial honey
Nights into tiny orbs of light,
Nights into hot baths outside in winter
Inside of carved out boulders found on the side of the road
Stars hovering over mountains
Until the cold air cools the water
Sends you shivering
To hot baths inside where you share
Each of your returning visuals for
The metaphor of life
Yours is a squished up celery dream
A dream on rewind
Like unzipping a mouth
You try to explain
Until words dissolve from water
To steam

    Celery strands to
       clothesline
  tea kettle to
     rose
        scissors
            to
               kiss.

www.ingramcontent.com/pod-product-compliance
Lightning Source LLC
LaVergne TN
LVHW040116080426
835507LV00041B/1109